O'Carolan

for Classical Guitar

Lyrical Harp Pieces
for Guitar Solo

Guido Böger

Grand Concert Brazilian guitar by Pimentel Guitars, Albuquerque, New Mexico, USA.

WWW.MELBAY.COM

Foreword

With this fourth edition, my arrangements of the 214 melodies of Turlough O'Carolan (1670-1738) are now complete. Since his pieces allow for a variety of possibilities as to harmony, secondary voices and ornamentation, I hope these arrangements can join the ongoing global engagement with O'Carolan's works.

Once again, I must thank my wife, Margaret Ellen Fitzgerald, for her support and feedback, as well as the many musical and stylistic suggestions she contributed in preparing this volume.

Guido Böger

Remarks:

1. The tempo and character markings at the beginning of the pieces reflect those used in the standard printed editions of these works.

2. Exactly which of the many versions of "Cock up Your Beaver" (i.e., put your beaver fur (felt) hat on at a jaunty angle) O'Carolan used as the basis for his variations has not been recorded. In the beginning of my arrangement, I used as the theme a combination of various versions of the air, as found in editions from the 18th and 19th centuries. Starting in measure 9, I quoted the version found in James Johnson's *Scots Musical Museum* (published in 1792), the only difference being the addition of a bass line of my own. Unlike O'Carolan's version, I used a 6/4 time signature.

In "When She Cam Ben" I also adapted the time signature of the variations into a 6/8, except for the last variation, which is presented here in its original 6/8 time, but was later transformed into the relative 6/16 time.

3. In the cases where different melodies share identical names or titles, I have included the piece's number, as presented in the O'Sullivan edition of O'Carolan's tunes.

4. The time change in "Mrs. O'Connor" reflects the phrasing at that point.

5. Appogiaturas: Grace notes should generally be played before the beat, as short anticipatory figures.
   a) Without a rest, they are attached to the note of the upper/lower voice, respectively.
   b) With a rest, they are separated from the note of the upper/lower voice.

Contents

Colonel O'Hara

Turlough O'Carolan
1670-1738

Allegretto

18
II
22
26
29
31
12

O'Flinn

Turlough O'Carolan

Colonel Manus O'Donnell

Turlough O'Carolan

Allegretto

21
②
VIII
VII
②
②
III
25
29
③

Mr. O'Connor

Turlough O'Carolan

Allegro moderato

V
I
VII
VII
V
V

Jig

John O'Connor

Turlough O'Carolan

Allegretto

Mrs. O'Connor

Turlough O'Carolan

Hugh O'Donnell

Turlough O'Carolan

Vivace

Sir Edward Crofton

Turlough O'Carolan

James Crofton

Turlough O'Carolan

Andantino

Mrs. Crofton

Turlough O'Carolan

Andantino

Miss Crofton

Turlough O'Carolan

Andantino

Robert Jordan

Turlough O'Carolan

Moderato

17
20
23
gliss.
26
II
29
31

II
V
c.f.

49
II
V
52
II
II
II
port.
55
gliss.
c.f.
58
c.f.
61
II
63
II
V

John Jones

Turlough O'Carolan

Con moto

V
VII

41
II
45
49
53
57
61

Carolan's Draught

Turlough O'Carolan

Andante con moto

John Moore

Turlough O'Carolan

Andante con moto

Jig
più mosso

Mrs. O'Neill of Carlane

Turlough O'Carolan

Allegretto

Mrs. O'Neill

Turlough O'Carolan

Conor O'Reilly

Turlough O'Carolan

Owen O'Rourke

Turlough O'Carolan

Andante con moto

Mrs. O'Rourke

Turlough O'Carolan

Andante

Frank Palmer

Turlough O'Carolan

Squire Parsons

Turlough O'Carolan

Andante con moto

John Peyton

Turlough O'Carolan

Moderato

Eleanor Plunkett

Turlough O'Carolan

Andantino

Mervyn Pratt

Turlough O'Carolan

Allegretto

David Power

Turlough O'Carolan

41
44
47
50
II
52
VII

George Reynolds

Turlough O'Carolan

Allegretto

Lady St. John

Turlough O'Carolan

Moderato

Mrs. Sterling

Turlough O'Carolan

Moderato

Major Shanley

Turlough O'Carolan

Andante con moto

25
gliss.
29
gliss.
33
37
41

Captain Sudley or Carolan's Dowry

Turlough O'Carolan

Moderato

21
II
II
II
25
V
29
III
II

General Wynne

Turlough O'Carolan

Tempo di marcia

Jig

William Ward

Turlough O'Carolan

Allegretto

Lady Wrixon

Turlough O'Carolan

Allegretto

Mr. Malone

Turlough O'Carolan

26
30
34
I
38
X

Margaret Malone

Turlough O'Carolan

Planxty Wilkinson

Turlough O'Carolan

Moderato

Carolan's Quarrel with the Landlady

Turlough O'Carolan

Con fuoco

Carolan's Cap

Turlough O'Carolan

Giocoso

Carolan's Cottage

Turlough O'Carolan

Andante

Blind Mary

Turlough O'Carolan

Andante

21
25
IV
29
33
gliss.

The Dark, Plaintive Youth

Turlough O'Carolan

Moderato

The Elevation

Turlough O'Carolan

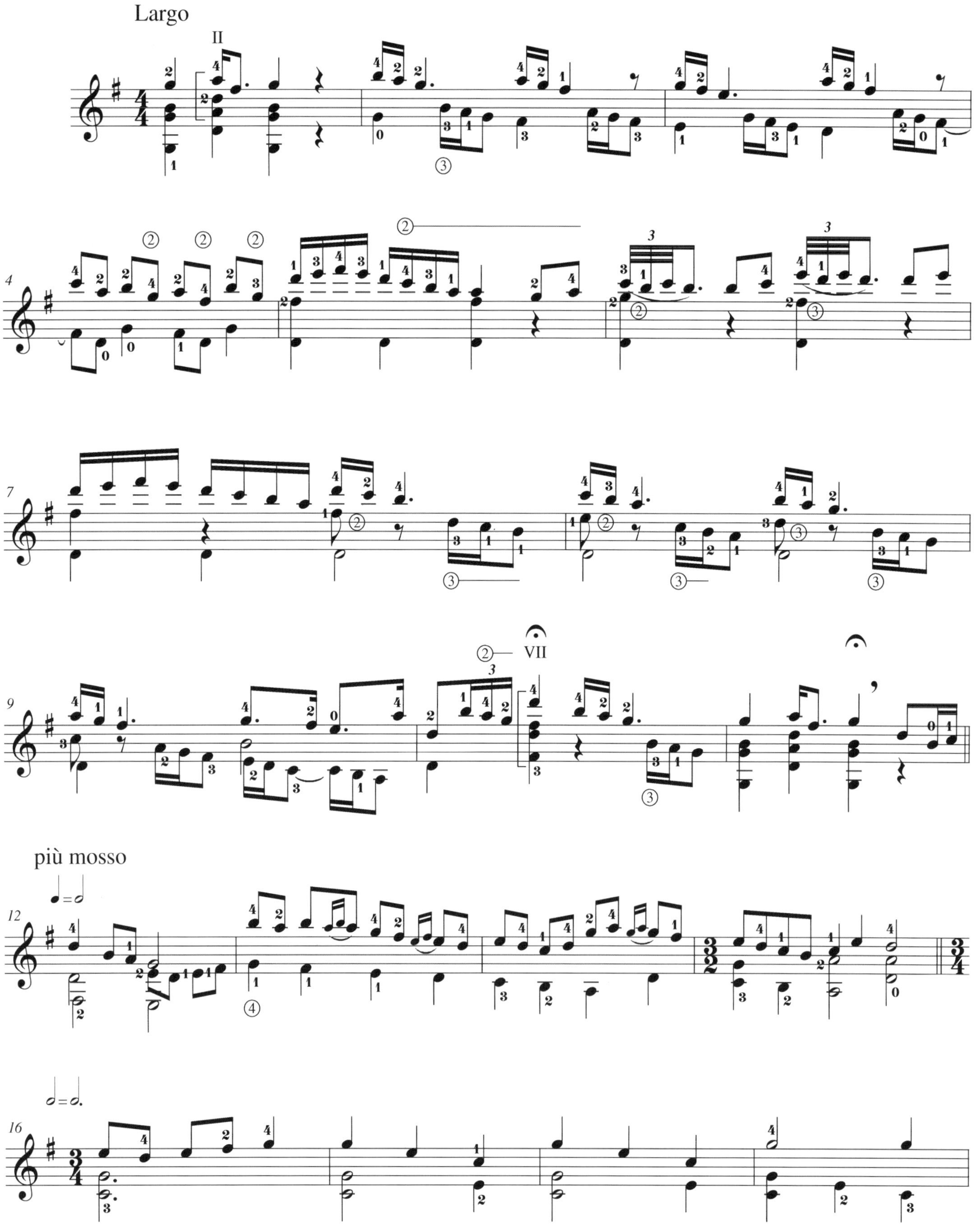

II
VII
III
III
V
III
a piacere
gliss.

The Fairy Queen

Turlough O'Carolan

Andante con moto

33
38
43
49
54
59

II
II
8va
8va
8va
8va
12
ritardando

The Seas Are Deep

Turlough O'Carolan

Adagio

The Landlady

Turlough O'Carolan

Vivace ma non troppo

21
25
29
33
37

The Two William Davises

Turlough O'Carolan

Moderato

Captain O'Neill

Turlough O'Carolan

Planxty by Carolan

Originally Untitled (173)

attributed to Turlough O'Carolan

Allegro comodo

Planxty O'Neill

Originally Untitled

attributed to Turlough O'Carolan

A Planxty
Originally Untitled (175)

attributed to Turlough O'Carolan

Allegretto grazioso

23
27
32
IV
5 or 24
8va

Planxty Browne

Originally Untitled

attributed to Turlough O'Carolan

Vivace

II
VII
II

Planxty by Carolan

Originally Untitled (172)

attributed to Turlough O'Carolan

Poco andante

Planxty Safaigh

attributed to Turlough O'Carolan

Moderato

III

Variations on "Cock up Your Beaver"

Variations attributed
to Turlough O'Carolan

Allegretto

(Variations)

43
46
49
II
1.
2.
52
54
II
56
II
59
1.
2.

61
64
1.
2.
68
71
II
73
ritardando

Variations on the Scottish Air

"When She Cam Ben"

Variations attributed to
Turlough O'Carolan

III
gliss.
gliss.
III

49
53
57
III
63
gliss.
(Air)
65
70

Planxty Scott

Originally Untitled

attributed to Turlough O'Carolan

Carolan's Maggot*

Turlough O'Carolan

*An odd fancy or whim.

About the Author

Guido Böger

The guitarist Guido Böger was born and raised in Bad Lippspringe, North-Rhine Westphalia, Germany. He became interested in the classical guitar and its music in his youth, learning a variety of classical as well as popular literature. He was later admitted into the Cologne College of Music, where he majored in classical guitar. Through later studies, he then completed the "Reifeprüfung" (the German Master of Music Degree in Performance) at the Music College of Aachen, Germany.

In addition to his teaching commitments at area music schools, including the University of Paderborn, Germany, he performs in numerous concerts both as a soloist, and in a variety of chamber music capacities. In 1993, Guido was featured on the CD *Hexachord–New Music for Two Guitars*. Since 1994, he has also performed regularly with his wife, the soprano Meg Fitzgerald, as the Duo "Chitarra Canta", presenting a variety of art song, Celtic and jazz-classics programs. In 2001 they recorded the CD *Aisling - Irish Art Songs & Music*.

Through the demands of this concert work, he began writing more arrangements for voice and guitar, as well as solo settings of various music styles for the guitar. In recent years, Guido has released a collection of his arrangements of German Lieder for voice and guitar, *Und Wüssten's die Blumen...* from works by Fanny (Mendelssohn) Hensel, with Furore Editions of Kassel, Germany, as well as having worked with the modern German composer Günther Becker in editing his "Vier Studien" (Four Etudes) for solo guitar, with Edition Gravis, in Brühl, Germany.

Guido Böger began working with Mel Bay Publications, Inc. in 2002 and, since the release of the first volume in 2010, has concluded his series of arrangements of the complete harp works of Turlough O'Carolan for classical guitar in 2022.

Other Mel Bay Classic Guitar Books